time management

& organizatio
(and th

an organized student means less stress, more free time, and better grades!

about the author!!!

Amy (Shwartzstein) Morris

Amy is a Massachusetts native and a graduate of George Washington University. With a degree in accounting, Amy worked in the financial and securities trading business for a number of years, holding senior management positions at Coopers and Lybrand; Price Waterhouse; Cantor Fitzgerald, New York; and Cantor Fitzgerald, London. Since leaving the corporate world, Amy has engaged herself in several projects including her recent launching of Got Family? Get Organized! © website and previous bestselling book, Got Kids? Get Organized! ©.

Got Kids? Get Organized! © is the original paper-folio organizer. Both allow all types of information—from school schedules and extracurricular activities and social events to sports team information and medical and travel information—all to be stored and easily be accessed.

Got Family? Get Organized! © combines Amy's organizational expertise, business savvy, and entrepreneurial drive into an online, at-a-glance, organizer that is designed to keep up with the increasingly complex needs of today's busy families.

The difference? Got Kids? Get Organized! © is organized in one central book, while Got Family? Get Organized! © can be accessed anytime and anywhere—from a computer.

Amy currently resides, happily ever organized, in Boca Raton, Florida.

For my children, Jessica and Matthew, without you this book would not be possible. Being your mom is a dream come true every day. Thank you for your continuous support, and for letting me know that yes, we can do it, even if it is just the three of us.

Acknowledgements:

Thank you to everyone who has supported my idea of bringing this book to life. It has been a passion of mine to teach what comes naturally to me and my children to everyone. Jill, my editor, and Jon, my graphic designer – it was an amazing experience. Karen, you are by far my favorite and most valued second set of eyes. And finally, a special thank you to my mom and dad. You have taught me to achieve what I set out to do, and you have been there every step of the way. Dad the countless hours you put in to help me read and edit and reread and reedit were immeasurable. We make a great team. I love you both very much.

Batman couldn't save anyone if his utility belt was a big messy bag full of broken pencils and candy wrappers. Instead, it was always super organized—making it easy to find his Batarang, his Cutting Torch, or his Smoke Pellets. Being organized means knowing where important items are, and knowing where to put them when you are done so you can find them again when you need them. What if batman's Jumpline Gun was lost in the bottom of his backpack and it took him fifteen minutes to find it? That would never work!

An Overview...

"Organization cannot make a genius out of an incompetent; on the other hand, disorganization can scarcely fail to result in efficiency." – *Dwight D. Eisenhower*

In school, students are rarely taught how to organize. For many people, the tendency to organize does not come naturally; it is something that must be taught, practiced, and maintained. Organizing your locker at the beginning of the year is worthwhile, but if it is not maintained, it quickly devolves into a mess, and the purpose is defeated.

Becoming organized is an AWESOME OPPORTUNITY for students to feel confident and independent. They will be less likely to lose their sanity and you can keep yours, too! Organization is the key ingredient in structuring an efficient life. Learning how to organize at a young age is an asset—not only for school, but in every aspect of life.

Time Management & Organizational Skills for Students is divided into two areas:

Section 1:

The first section is for parents—it provides them with an understanding of why time management is important from the earliest grades through middle school, high school, college, and into their own adult lives. Not only will this section introduce the concepts, it will also provide guidelines to help your child become organized (and maybe you, too!)

Section 2:

The second section is geared for the student audience. It provides similar explanations as to why organization and time management is important to success throughout their school years. It gives examples of how to attain the goal of learning to be organized, and how to maintain it.

NOTE:

Please note that adults should also read section two as many of these same suggestions apply to their daily routine.

REMEMBER:

- **Organization is a team effort!**
- **It requires good communication amongst all family members.**
- **With everyone on board, there is mutual reinforcement.**

Organizing never stops, no matter your age, the size of your home, whether you work or not, whether your house is full of kids or you are an empty nester. Keep on organizing and always look for new ways to improve both your organizing skills and your organization methods. Helpful hints are continuously available on the GotFamilyGetOrganized website blog, and new ideas are always welcome additions.

ORGANIZE, STAY ORGANIZED, AND ORGANIZE EVEN BETTER! YOU CAN'T GO WRONG.

CONTENTS...

For the Parent!!!

For the Student!!!

Extra! Extra!!!

* Throughout this document, references to "child," "children," "student," "students," "them," "their," "his," or "hers," are used interchangeably to bring some variety to the text. As applicable, it may refer to a single child or children, regardless of gender, to be understood in the environment of the topic discussed.

THERE ARE ONLY 24 HOURS IN A DAY...
and you and your family have to sleep sometime!

"Good order is the foundation of all things." – Edmund Burke,
Whig Party, Great Britain House of Commons

Whether in elementary school, middle school, high school or college, all students have essentially the same amount of hours – give or take, depending on small scheduling differences – to manage their school work, extracurricular activities and normal daily routine.

Here Are Some Thoughts And Things To Consider:

 If we manage ourselves and organize our tasks and goals, **we accomplish more**.

 If we are disorganized it becomes hard to accomplish what we set out to do.

 The net result of being organized, besides the obvious benefits, is **a great sense of satisfaction** in knowing that YOU are in control.

 A pitfall to be wary of is over-scheduling. There is one significant limit to self-organization. It's similar to the old adage of trying to put 2 pounds of flour into a one pound bag; NO AMOUNT OF ORGANIZATION WILL OVERCOME HAVING MORE TO DO IN THE AMOUNT OF TIME AVAILABLE TO DO IT! Don't take on too much. Know when to say no if it takes time that you don't have to do it – whatever "it" is.

 We can help our children select and prioritize goals that will lead to better organization of time, completion of goals, creation of more free time, and a greater feeling of success and independence.

 If parents set an example by being organized and following good time management techniques, chances are the child is likely to follow suit.

 Having an efficient routine will cut out wasted time. For example, plan car trips to pick up the kids at sporting events and play dates so you are not traversing the same route twice.

 Creating and following a well-planned schedule will significantly reduce or even eliminate frustration and anxiety.

IT PAYS!!
BENEFITS TO BEING ORGANIZED...

"A first rate organizer is never in a hurry. He is never late. He always keeps up his sleeve a margin for the unexpected." – Arnold Bennett, English Novelist

Getting organized isn't going to seem important to your child just because you tell them it is. However, if you explain the following six benefits—giving them examples from their own experiences—they will be more likely to grasp the concept and engage in being organized.

1. More Free Time!!!

 You'll spend less time looking for lost or misplaced items and less time cramming at the last minute for exams. You're organized life will lead to the discovery of more free time!

 You won't be late. Being organized can help you get "out the door" on time!

2. Saving Money!!!

 You will no longer need to replace items you thought were missing or lost due to disorganization!

 You will no longer need to replace ruined items left in the wrong place, which broke or became dammaged.

3. Less Stress!!!

 Disorganization causes so many tears and so much stress!

 Arriving at school in a good mood makes for a cheerful and ready-to-begin-the-day student.

 Being organized allows you to get out the door with fewer arguments.

4. Fewer Scheduling Conflicts!!!

 Being organized reduces the amount of "double booking" of time or missing an appointment that someone forgot to put it on the calendar.

5. Self-Sufficiency!!!

 Being organized will help give your kids a new level of independence and will help them feel more in-control of their day and their lives—and less dependent on you to make things happen for them.

6. Empower Your Student!!!

 By learning organizational skills at an early age, kids will already have the tools they need to feel in control throughout their lives—as students, young adults at work, and as parents, themselves.

GOT TIME?
THE TYPICAL 24-HOUR WEEKDAY...

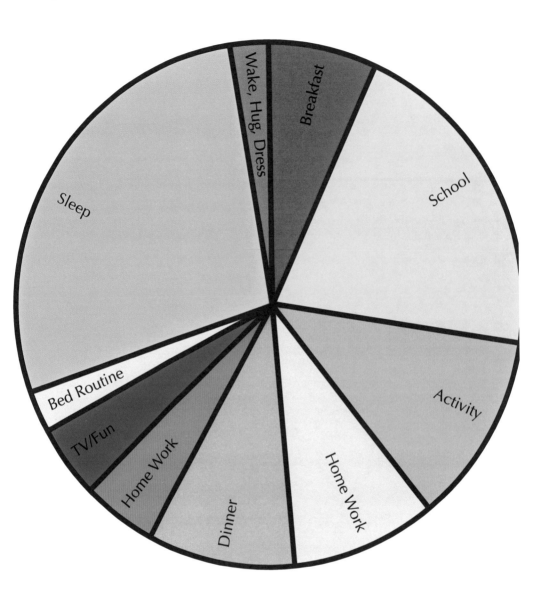

Most children have the same basic weekday routine—the same 24 hours to complete their goals. At least 180 school days each year are spent following the same general routine.

Morning Routine
- Wake
- Hygiene – Wash Up. Brush Teeth and Hair
- Dress
- Make Bed and Cleanup Room.
- Breakfast – Eat a good breakfast. Food feeds the brain!

School
- Classes
- Physical Activity
- Homework Assignments

Afterschool Activity
- Music, Art, Dance Classes
- Sports – Practices, Games
- Job
- Volunteer Work
- Social Time

Evening Routine
- Homework/Study Time
- Dinner
- Hygiene
- Bedtime

It is important to note that homework, study and dinner time are in no particular order as some children prefer to get homework done right after school while others prefer to wait until after dinner. This can vary based on school and activity schedules as well as the personal preference of what works best for each child.

Helping your child to figure out what order works best for them will be important when building their daily and/or weekly schedules. This will be discussed in greater detail in PLANNING AND CREATING A SCHEDULE.

Additional Tips For Waking Up And Getting To Bed:
- Awaken children at the same time every morning.
- Set an alarm clock with time to spare.
- If you have a snoozer child, set two alarm clocks and put one in a location where your child MUST get out of bed to turn it off.
- Try to have children in bed at the same time every night; and try to follow the same routine.

"Don't agonize, organize." – Florynce Kennedy, Civil Rights Advocate and Feminist

★ A tidy room means finding things easily with less yelling and frustration!

★ Planning school projects in advance means less pressure just before a project is due!

★ Remembering to bring a soccer uniform or dance clothes to school means going to practice or dance class straight from school— without a meltdown!

Let's Talk About It!

Helping children set goals—both immediate and long term—and making a plan to achieve them is one important long-term benefit of being organized. The first step is to involve your child in a discussion about their interests. Then you can talk about the goals for getting everything they want in their schedules. Let them help shape their time. If they are involved in the process, there is a greater chance they'll take ownership of their time and schedule.

This discussion can include:

✔ Exploring options for upcoming activities.

✔ Encouraging them to stay busy with what really interests them while still leaving room in their schedules to try something new.

✔ Reminding them (and you, too) that it's not necessary for every hour of the day to be filled with activity.

✔ Helping them realize that while some children function better with more activity, other like less. (There is a fine balance between being active and being over-committed and overwhelmed.) For those who do prefer and can handle a hectic schedule, it is even more crucial that they stay organized. Remember, being busy does not necessarily equate to being productive.

✔ Building in free time and fun in your child's schedule.

An Example: Learning Piano

Let's say your child tells you that he or she wants to play piano. Learning to play requires lessons and practice time. Before running out and signing up, you should break down the time commitment into segments with your child, and understand what will be required for lessons and for practice each week.

Help them realize that there is a "time" component to each piece:

- Lessons may take thirty minutes each week and depending on whether the lesson is at home or not will determine the amount of preparation time.
- Realize that a thirty-minute lesson could amount to a sixty-minute block of time. Do the same for practice.
- Depending on the student, practice could mean as much as fifteen to forty-five minutes a day or as little as a few times a week.

We've Chosen Our Activities! Now what?

After determining the amount of time it takes to accomplish each activity, choose a block of time for each one. Let your child help determine when; what day and what time during the day. Are they better at practicing right after school? After dinner? Or just before bed-time? Ultimately you want your child to be able to get the job done on their own versus following the schedule you determine for them. However, as the adult, you should guide the process. You may not want your child practicing piano at 6:00 a.m.! Keep times for activities consistent each day. Having a consistent routine will help children manage their time and accomplish more. Remember: if your child helps in the decision making process; it is more likely he or she will take ownership of these commitments.

REMINDER:
Everyone Needs a Break. Don't Forget About Down Time!

Remember:

Kids are at school all day; and in most cases it is unrealistic to expect they will come home and do homework immediately. Like adults, they need and crave down time. Physical activity is a great way to expend energy – it could also be a quiet activity they choose (such as drawing or reading) if they are not interested in active play. Make sure to schedule downtime—and always make sure there is time for it in your week!

ONE BLOCK AT A TIME...
planning and creating a schedule

"A sense of the value of time – that is, of the best way to divide one's time into one's various activities – is an essential preliminary to efficient work; it is the only method of avoiding hurry."
– Arnold Bennett, English Poet

Our Kids see their teachers and parents using schedules all the time.

They see us referring to date books or mobile-phone calendars. Kids understand that it's good to write things down! Nowadays, schools even supply students with daily planners. They're helping students get off on solid footing. Using a planner is a tool for life. Helping your child structure their day and week makes it easier for the whole family to get things done and will help to make life feel less stressful.

Start By Selecting A Chart!

Choose a weekly calendar, a monthly calendar, a student planner, a spreadsheet, or a simple chart you make from hand. Give your child several options, and have them select which one feels more comfortable or appealing. However, it is recommended that students in the sixth grade and higher us a student planner or weekly calendar for scheduling. Whichever tool your child selects, the spaces need to be big enough to write in.

Fill In All Of Your Scheduled Activities.

Examples include sports practices and games, art classes, music classes, and any other scheduled activity. (Note: medically necessary routines should also be considered an activity).

> For younger school-aged children a simple chart is a wonderful tool.
> **Get them involved!**
> 1. Ask your child to take a pencil and mark the day's start time and end time. These times will vary based on your child's age and your family's rules.
> 2. Once you're child's schedule is determined, go over each day, and ask him/her to fill in the calendar with day and time for each regularly-scheduled activity. Help your child to write in or draw a picture of the activity in the blocked out time slot. Some activities are daily, some weekly, some monthly, etc., so you will want to note this on the schedule to avoid confusion.

Block Out The Rest:

Once scheduled activities are on the calendar, you will be able to clearly see what times are available for homework, studying, play, and any other activities. Try to estimate when these other activities will take place and how much time each involves, then block them out on your schedule.

Keep Those Piles Of Calendars
And Announcements Around:

Schools, extracurricular classes, and sports teams send out calendars. Hold onto these until you have copied the schedule into your planner. You may also decide you want to keep them on hand in a folder or hang them on a bulletin board for reference until the season or session is over.

DON'T FORGET THINGS CHANGE . . .
Make sure to review and update events and activities that come up—including club meetings, teacher conferences, tutoring, and doctors' appointments. Also fill in specific events, including project and report due dates, recitals, social engagements, and sporting events.

Scheduling In Wellness:

If your child is on long- or short-term medication, it will be important to make time in your schedule for administering it. In the case of a long- or short-term medical condition, there may be office visits, dietary needs, and appliances or equipment needed to assist your child with everyday activities.

You'll want to approach filling in your planner with these needs in mind. For example, taking medication might be scheduled under "hygiene." Another option: put it in a section "before" or "after" school activities. This way, medicine and other wellness needs are built into the schedule. Making wellness part of your child's every-day schedule will make the activity feel like any other part of the day—and will contribute to positive feelings and healthy self-esteem. The goal here is very similar to the other organizational techniques. You want your child to feel independent, in control, and in the case of a medical condition or physical disability—not too hampered by having to schedule in extra necessities each day.

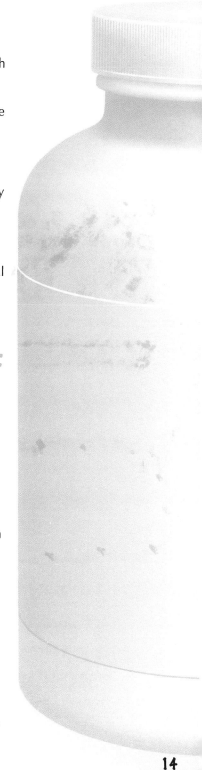

Additional Tips For Younger Children:

Get Into A Routine!
A daily routine will help a younger child to REMEMBER because they become accustomed to doing the same thing every day.

Make A Chart:
Younger children love charts! Make one and hang it on their bathroom or bedroom door. They'll learn to read the words and identify with pictures telling them to brush teeth, get dressed, put dirty clothing in the hamper, flush the toilet, and anything else.

Reward Little Ones:
Use stickers daily to reward them for completing tasks from their chart. Or even better—give a bigger treat at the end of the week after they have completed an entire week's worth of tasks.

And Try Not To Forget:
They are children and perfection should not be expected, so be enthusiastic and positive. This is a learning lesson.

ORGANIZING YOUR SPACE...
be ready to get out the door with everything you need!

Score 1 For The Home Team:

**Head out the door with everything you need...
including your child!**

Avoid the morning panic. School mornings are hectic by nature. Instead of scrambling for last night's homework and today's sports equipment while packing a lunch and eating breakfast, try to prepare the night before!

✔ Look at your child's schedule with them or have your teen look at their schedule for the next day and get everything ready and placed by the door.

✔ Get clothes ready – decide on your outfit and place the clothes for easy dressing in the morning.

✔ Make sure all parent notes and signed papers are in the right place to go back to school.

✔ Get backpacks, homework, sports equipment, library books, etc., ready.

✔ Prepare lunch and snacks.

Papers! Papers! Papers!

The amount of information exchanged between home and school beginning late summer and continuing throughout the school year is massive. There are forms to be completed for emergency contact information, emergency medical information, general "tell-us-about-your-child" questionnaires, immunization records, athletic participation and physicals, and possibly even more. Plus there are the mounds of papers that come home during the year – field trip permission slips, progress and report cards, flyers for events such as bake sales, sports, dance and charity events, just to name a few. Papers! The flow is never ending.

Organized communal spaces that enable efficient and stress free time management make it easier on everyone in the home to find what they need when they need it and stay organized. Additionally, it will help in the scheduling process and help avoid double booking of activities or other scheduling conflicts.

Mudroom

The "mud room," as it has been dubbed in my home, is our central spot for dropping keys, backpacks, coats, shoes, briefcases, and any item used daily. The size of your home and the space you have available will determine how and where a mudroom can be arranged most efficiently. Ideally it should be located nearest to the entry/exit door used most often.

What You Will Need For Your Mudroom:

Key items you'll need include coat hooks, baskets, a table or piece of furniture with drawers, a shallow bowl for collecting loose change, built in locker-style cubbies, small hooks for keys, a shoe sorter and a small basket to collect outgoing mail.

What Else?

If space allows, you can add additional small storage baskets, stacking trays, hanging pockets, or bowls for outgoing permission slips, daily to- do list to grab on your way out, for items to be "read," "signed," "returned," and "recorded" or other items. Hang a magnetic or cork bulletin board and use it to tack up invitations, sports rosters and schedules, and to do notes. Kids love to see and collect invitations and it doubles as a visual reminder to purchase gifts.

What If I Have No Room?

If space is a concern and you don't have the option to create a mudroom, consider using a hall closet and reconfiguring the inside to include hanging space, hooks for backpacks on the side walls or inside the door, and shelves for basket storage. Use the space you have efficiently to gain the most storage potential for an organized "in and out the door" dumping area. This is how you will reduce clutter.

The Family Calendar

Have one family calendar for important events. Color-code calendar events by assigning each member of the family a different color pen or marker to write down/keep track of their items. Record all practices, games, club meetings, lessons, recitals, school vacation days, family birthdays, and anything else, in the calendar so that each family member can tell what the others have planned. They can then plan and organize their schedules with the knowledge they need. For family members that are color challenged, use shapes to distinguish that person's event from others. In front of the activity use a shape, such as a triangle or a bullet point.

Make sure to update the calendar immediately upon receiving new information, making additions and deletions, as necessary, and be mindful of ongoing activities from one month to the next.

To Do List

IT TAKES TWO TO TANGO...
help your student get organized

In the future, maybe technology will provide us with a means to remember everything we need to do without having to remind ourselves over and over. How frustrating to realize you've just returned from the supermarket without milk or butter! How hard is it for a kid who spent hours on an assignment, only to realize it's sitting on his desk at home and he's in school? Organization is best learned by following another's good example. Work with your children to help them to get organized.

First Thing On My List: Making A List!

Making lists is a key timesaving step in staying organized. If your child makes (and uses) lists, he will be able to see his accomplishments as he completes them. What's more satisfying than writing a "to do" item and then crossing it off when it's completed? And what's a better way to keep track of the items in life that need attention?

For younger children, you can help them make their list and let them cross off items as they complete them. You can also use stickers to indicate a task is complete. Younger children enjoy the visual reward. A list of "lists" is in the student section.

Time To Do Homework

The perfect homework space won't be the same for every child. Personality and age are factors that can help guide your decision. In every case, a workspace should be quiet, well-lit, and in a comfortable place. However, don't make it too comfortable; you don't want your child napping in their books when they have work to finish.

Younger children who are starting to work independently will often find the kitchen or dining room table a great homework space. It is centrally located and in close proximity by to Mom, Dad, nanny, babysitter or a grandparent—who can offer help if needed. A note about posture: It is important for the younger student to sit correctly in an ergonomically appropriate chair or placing a stool or crate at their feet in order to avoid developing bad habits—including poor posture and slouching.

Once a homework space is found, the space should be organized with the necessary tools needed to complete assignments: books, calculators, pens, pencils, crayons, paper, a computer and anything else your child would require to complete their homework assignments. Setting up a well organized desk or other study space is discussed in greater detail in the student section as well as storing exams and assignments completed during the school year.

Computer Files Without Tears

Nothing's worse for a child than the frustration of searching for a computer file that he knows he saved, but can't find. Well-organized computer files make it possible for your student to store and locate information without turning blue and shrieking.

An incidental benefit to file organization is when a child is not at home you can find something on the computer for him. Should he ask you to locate, print, or e-mail a document for him, a well-organized computer desktop and filing system facilitates fast, easy retrieval.

If your student has a computer of his own or uses the family computer, help him set up a place on the desktop where she can store her files—both for school and other activities. For every student in your household, make sure each has their own file storage space on whatever computer they use. You can follow the guideline in the student section for doing this effectively.

The Skinny On Backpacks

Choosing The Right Backpack:

Choosing the right backpack is just as important as an organizing it. When used correctly, backpacks are designed to distribute their weight to our strongest muscles. However, incorrectly-sized or poorly-used backpacks can lead to long term injury. A child may encounter muscle and joint injuries in the neck, back and shoulders, as well as bad posture.

Advice From A Professional:

Pamela Smith, a licensed and registered Occupational Therapist, in Poughkeepsie, NY, recommends the following:

 Backpack weight should be no more than 10% overall body weight.

 Purchase a backpack with wide, foam padded, adjustable, shoulder straps that can be tightened such that the backpack is secure and closely fit to the body. You do not want the backpack swinging around or hanging down on the child's shoulder.

 Purchase a backpack with two shoulder straps versus one, and use both straps at all times to equally distribute the weight and take the stress off of either shoulder.

 Look for a backpack that has a padded back as well as shoulder straps. It will save the body from being stabbed by stray, sharp objects.

 Consider a rolling backpack or a lightweight backpack for children who tend to carry a lot of weight on a regular basis.

AND THAT'S NOT ALL...

Lockers, student computer files, and other student items that require organization are discussed in greater detail in the Student Section.

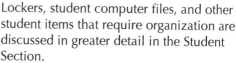

"It's always important to make your child feel they are being helpful and adding to the family, organization is a great way of saying, "look what you did, that is so helpful." Complimenting your child on a job well done goes a long way. – Karen M.

Parent Notes:

DEAR STUDENT -
A NOTE TO THE STUDENT:

"The five essential entrepreneurial skills for success are concentration, discrimination, organization, innovation and communication." – Michael Faraday, English Chemist and Physicist

Getting organized sounds hard, but it will make you less grouchy, faster on your feet, and more successful. It also means less stress, better grades, and more free time! Plus, you'll be able to find your stuff more easily!

Most of us aren't taught how to organize ourselves in the elementary grades. During those years, much organizing is done for us by our parents and teachers. This changes a lot when we reach middle school, junior high school, high school, and eventually college. These are the years—from about ages 10 to 22—when we are expected to know how to use basic organizational skills. Organization is not something that comes naturally to all of us, but it is a skill that can be learned. Once learned, it should be practiced and maintained.

The Benefits Are Many...

As an organized student, you will feel not only less stress, get better grades, and have more time. You will also gain the respect of your parents and teachers because you are together and efficient while feeling less out of control, gaining confidence, and earning independence.

Being Organized Means...

❀ More time hanging with friends, watching your favorite shows, making phone calls, being online, and ...

❀ More time in the mornings to get out the door! Less stress and feeling rushed because you can't find what you need.

❀ Less cramming for tests.

❀ Less money spent to replace lost or misplaced items.

❀ Less money spent to replace ruined items.

❀ Fewer arguments over the "small" stuff.

❀ Independence.

❀ Empowerment.

It is important to realize that being organized is not something you should expect to do overnight. Have realistic goals for what you want to accomplish; organizing your locker, your study space, your schedule, etc. Then, make a list and tackle each item individually and separately until everything is complete. Organization then becomes an eleven-letter word: MAINTENANCE! If you do not maintain the organization systems you set up for yourself, they quickly become confusing and dysfunctional, their purposes defeated and the benefits are no longer realized.

GETTING IT ALL DOWN IN ONE PLACE...
Scheduling

"Organizing is what you do before you do something, so that when you do it, it's not all mixed up."
- A. A. Milne, author of Winnie-the-Pooh

Choose The Right Planner Or Date Book For You.
The first thing you need to have is a planner. Is yours a book? A Week-at-a Glance®? An app or the calendar on your I-phone, Blackberry ®, or other PDA electronic device? Is it an old fashioned calendar with a daily joke or inspiration? Maybe it's the free planner school gives you, sponsored by the PTA? In any case, it's time to use it!

Why Should I Use A Planner?
You need to use a planner (or spreadsheet, or whatever you choose) because it's like having a brain outside of your body. If you use it, it will always "know" where you are supposed to be and doing. It's where you will keep your schedule: school assignments, vacation days, appointments, club meetings, athletics and any commitments you have.

One Location? Really?
Really! Recording everything in one location will make it possible (not just easy!) for you to know where you need to be; when and with what. However, you must update it regularly! Add, delete, make changes—or it won't be as useful. Your schedule is your master bible, your assistant, your brain—all in one—and if it is not up-to-date, you won't be either.

Now How Do I Do This?
During the school day, record each assignment as it is assigned. Add any other commitments such as newspaper club meetings, soccer or softball schedule changes, and music or dance lessons and practices. Try using different colors! If you use blue for sports and red for homework, you will more easily distinguish at-a-glance between assignment and activity type. Black, blue and red pens will work fine! It does not require a rainbow of fancy colors.

Now How Do I Do This? Now Use It!

Like Your Cell Phone, You Will Become Addicted to Something that Helps You.

Check your calendar each evening. Review your schedule for the following day and prepare what you will need. Preparing the night before—packing bags, organizing homework, putting athletic clothes and equipment in backpack—reduces stress, arguments, and time wasted getting out the door the following morning.

Notes

BE ORGANIZED AT HOME...

Homework Space: Where Should I Do My Homework?

This depends on how old you are and on what helps you to be your most productive. Important for most kids is that it should be a quiet, well-lit and comfortable space—although not too comfortable, you don't want to fall asleep in your books! A bed seems like a comfortable place to do reading, but the pillow and blanket may be too tempting. A chair with table for a glass of soda pop or water is better than a bed. A table or desk is the best place for writing or using a laptop.

If you are in middle school or above, you may have several different places where you like to do your work. Try to return to the same places where you get the most work accomplished. Eventually this spot will make you feel successful. However, it is our recommendation that you use a desk that is set up specifically for you.

Declutter My Desk!

★ Your desk should NOT be a catch-all dumping ground.

★ Keep the surface clear so that there is ample space to do your homework.

★ Don't let papers stack up! Sort regularly and store. You never know when you may need to refer to them again during the school year; especially during midterm and final exam time.

★ Keep a few writing instruments plus a scissor and ruler in a simple cup, desk caddy, or "in-drawer" organizer.

★ Store extras such as infrequently used supplies, e.g., construction paper and reference books, sorted and placed in labeled storage bags placed in either a single bin or separately labeled bins, and stored in a nearby closet, armoire or bookshelf, or in a family storage area designated for supplies. If stored in open view, use a decorative container.

Homework - As A Verb!

Research, reports, reading. Maybe those are really the "Three R's!" A large part of your final grade comes from homework and exams, so good homework and study skills are key. Now that you know how to organize yourself—bringing home the right books and assignments—you can get to the meaty part of your at-home school life—homework!

Getting It Done The Organized Way!
Use This Checklist:

✔ **Pick the best space** to begin your homework.

✔ **Prioritize!** Estimate the time it will take to complete each assignment and then number assignments in the order they should be completed. Try to do the most difficult assignments first. Don't leave them for last. By then you'll be tired and it will be late.

✔ **Stick to a daily homework routine** based on your daily activity schedule.

✔ **Take breaks** (a few minutes for every 30 to 45 minutes of work).

✔ **Focus!** Turn off television, take off the headphones, avoid text messaging, phone conversations, computer chats and social media sites when doing homework unless you're communicating about an assignment.

✔ **Check off assignments when complete and put them away** so that they can be located and handed in. This is especially important as you enter the higher grades as not all classes meet every day.

✔ **Pack up backpacks when homework is complete** so that in the morning everything you need is ready to go.

✔ **For long term assignments—make suitable entries in your planner—** and then tackle in manageable pre-scheduled parts.

Finding Your Own Way

What Study Method Works Best For You?

Not every study method works for everyone and for every subject. Experiment with those listed below or create your own method to figure out what study shortcuts work best for you.

Homework techniques that may work for you:

☺ Use flashcards

☺ Use outlines

☺ Ask someone to quiz you

☺ Use mnemonic devices for memorization

☺ Highlight notes

☺ Read all directions

It is important to realize that studying is not limited to doing just the homework assignment. It may require taking notes on an assigned reading chapter, reviewing graphs, charts and tables, and doing additional practice problems to reinforce formula memorization and use. Additionally, keep a dictionary and thesaurus on hand, or save the location of websites that offer these tools in your "favorites" or "benchmarks" on your web browser.

"I like to rewrite my homework list when I get home and list them in order of longest or hardest to easiest and then I start with the hardest first." - Jessica F

"When preparing flashcards, write them by hand versus typing them on the computer. You are more likely to remember what you write than what you type." - Jessica S.

"I like to put a sticky note on each homework assignment to indicate its due date."—Megan S.

TAME THE PAPER PILE...FILE OR PILE?

Where Do My Papers Go?

Sorting school work, notes, and papers is crucial at exam time, especially if midterm and end of year final exams are cumulative. If you have lots of piles, your answer may be to try files. You will be happy when finished papers, notes, and exams are simple to put your hands on.

File It

There are various filing systems and several are suggested below:

Ever Heard Of Hanging Files?

Hanging files can go in a file cabinet, a plastic file storage container, or in a basic bankers/archive box. The hanging file can hold papers directly, or manila or colorful file folders with papers in them. Choose a filing system and buy what you need (hanging files and/or file folders) at the stationery or office supply store, or a discount retailer. You can buy a box of colored file folders to go inside your hanging files or your binder—one color for each subject instead of the plane manila folders for quicker identification of subjects.

The More Portable Choice—The Binder:

A binder is a useful system if you don't have room for hanging files. Consider using an expanding folder, binder, or a large paper or plastic envelope to store your materials. The binder is not the preferred method unless you can hole-punch all items to store them in an orderly way. The downside of using a binder/folder/plastic envelope system for filing is that you risk using a lot of pocket folders and "shoving" items into the binder without them being secure.

Now What?

You can use folders for different categories. If you choose hanging files, buy "insertable" clear plastic tabs and label a hanging file for each class. Depending on exam schedules and types or subject matter covered, it may be wise to create a folder within each category (or envelope) for the semester, trimester or syllabus topic. Your history file might contain folders such as First Semester Notes, First Semester Exams, and First Semester Quizzes, or alternatively, The Revolutionary War, The 13 Original Colonies, and so forth. After items are graded and assignments are completed, file them in their respective folders.

In What Order Do I File My Papers?

File your papers in reverse chronological order so that the most recent date are the first in view. Keep chapter and similar subject matter together using staples or paper/binder clips. Everything should be where you need it in order to study for cumulative tests. At the end of the year sort through and keep only what matters most.

The overall goal is to have all your papers on-hand and easily retrievable when needed, therefore reducing the amount of aggravation that could arise.

"One day I was too lazy to put my English packets away properly in my locker so I threw them out. Then at the end of the year the teacher said we could bring them in and use them as reference for the final exam. My final exam grade was lower than what it could have been because I did not have my materials and the teacher was not giving out more copies. I learned my lesson about filing my papers." -Brandon S.

UIRTUAL STORAGE...

Organizing Your Computer Desktop For Schoolwork

A good system for computer files makes it easy to store and locate information when you need it.

Step 1:
Create a master folder, and name it. You might call it School Folder or use your name, for example: Amy's School Folder.

Step 2:
Create a sub folder for each grade year under the master folder. For example: Sixth Grade, Seventh Grade, or Eleventh Grade.

Step 3:

As you receive a schedule of classes, create additional sub folders for each class. For example: English, Geometry, Music, Physics, or History.

Here's an example of how it will look showing the hierarchy of files and folders:

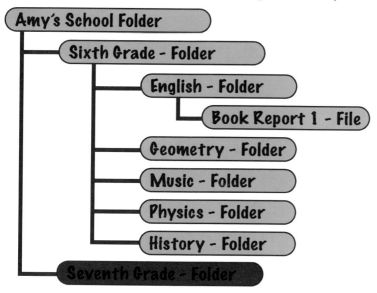

Step 4:

As you work on assignments, name your files to clearly identify the project, e.g., Colonial Day Paper. A good way to label a document or file in progress is to name it, for example, Book Report 1, Book Report 2, and so forth. You may also want to add a date or a version number. When you get to the final version, label it Book Report Final.

A TIP:

Try to save each draft version rather than saving over the original just in case you decide you need access to a prior version. Saving drafts can also help you if the file becomes corrupted. You'll still have some, if not all, of the work available on a previous version. SAVE OFTEN!!

REMEMBER:

Keeping track of your files in an organized manner is efficient, time saving, and very beneficial to staying organized.

BE ORGANIZED AT SCHOOL: THINK MARY POPPINS...

Backpack 911!

When you reach into your backpack, do you see old snack bags and candy wrappers? Do you feel liquid puddles? Can you find your books and notebooks?

Think of your backpack as your personal assistant. Think of Mary Poppins who could pull anything out of her bag in a snap. Whether the style of the backpack is a roll-pack, a big bag, or a traditional backpack, it should be organized neatly and contain only the items necessary for the school day. Use a separate bag for gym clothes and afterschool activities such as sport, music, and art.

Don'ts:

☹ No loose papers.

☹ No non-school materials.

☹ No junk.

☹ No liquids unless they are sealed well.

Dos:

☺ Use a case for writing instruments to avoid the awful mess when an explosion occurs.

☺ Label all items that belong to you with your name: books, notebooks, rulers, calculators, etc.

Do You Carry Your Backpack Around All Day?

If not, when you arrive at school in the morning, unload your books and notebooks and anything else into your locker and store your backpack until the end of the day.

At The End Of The Day, Remember What You Need To Bring Home!

At the end of the day, do the opposite. Check your planner as you are loading up, and then fill up your backpack with books, notebooks, calculators, permission slips, projects, and anything you will need at home. Remember to place books and the heaviest items at the center of the back for better weight distribution and carrying.

Until You Are Ready To Get To Work, Find A Spot For Your Backpack.

At home, fine one location for your backpack and school items. Using the same location each day is a good idea. Once you are ready to sort through your backpack and begin your evening routine, empty your books and notebooks and put them where you will be working.

Getting Down To Work Means A Little Clean Up First!

- Before you get to work, throw away trash and items that have managed to pile up in your backpack.
- Place permission slips or any papers your parent or guardian needs to read and/or sign in a designated location or a basket so that they are not lost and not forgotten about.
- Any loose papers that did not get placed in the correct notebooks or folders should be sorted out, hole-punched if needed and filed correctly.

Now Begin Hour Homework!

At the end of the evening, take the time to pack up your backpack and prepare for the next day of school. Review your planner for assignments, permission slips, books and projects needed. Prepare any gym and after school activity items as well. Place backpack and after school items by the door to go out.

In the morning, grab and go.

NOTE:
Not sure what type of backpack to use? Refer to the parent section for tips on choosing the right backpack.

Your Locker – Your School Closet

Does the mess in your locker remind you of the mess in your room? It's even worse because a locker is so tiny! Finding a book in a messy locker is the worse than looking for your keys.

Organizing and maximizing the small locker space you have will make it easier to find what you are looking for. You will save time and avoid the stress of not having what you need.

Why receive a lower grade or a zero on an assignment you can't locate?

Why miss a field trip because the permission slip was under an avalanche in your locker? Or maybe it wasn't! Maybe it's at home! Where is it?

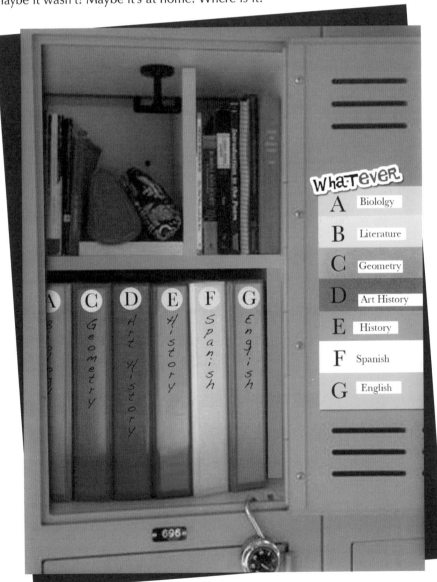

WhaTeveR

A Biololgy
B Literature
C Geometry
D Art History
E History
F Spanish
G English

Organize Your Locker:

- **Use shelves** to provide multiple levels of storage. If your locker is tall enough, stack two shelves.
- **Laminate a copy of your schedule**, and hang it on the inside of the locker door.
- **Keep a pencil case/pencil cup.**
- **Keep extra lined and graph paper and index cards.**
- **Use color or shapes to match books and notebooks by subject.** This will help you keep text books and notebooks together. Code by subject and try to be consistent from one year to the next. Color code or choose a shape to identify subjects. Draw the shape on a sticker that can be affixed to binders and folders and draw the shape on the book's binding. (Note: If folders are too large to keep with books on the lower locker shelf, place folders and binders together on the top shelf and leave books on the bottom shelf.)
- **Personalize your space** with pictures, a mirror, dry-erase board, etc.
- **Use a hanging locker organizer** for your cell phone, calculator and other items.
- **Load books you will need later into your backpack immediately following class.** At the end of the day, double check against your homework planner to make sure everything you need is packed up. If time does not allow, then list the books you'll need at the same time you write down the assignment in your planner. At the end of the day when you are loading up, check your list.
- **GIRLS will want to keep a personal kit in their locker** for extra hair bands, hygiene items, a spare pair of panties, tissues, lotions, and money for after school activity.
- **BOYS** keep a "just-in-case" kit with band aids, tissues, and money.
- **DON'T put open liquid items or open snack bags in your locker.**
- **DON'T keep expensive jewelry, valuable, or irreplaceable items in your locker.**
- **Keep hand sanitizer in your locker.**
- **Keep your locker LOCKED** and **NEVER share your combination.**
- **Record your locker's lock combination** in your cell phone just in case you forget it, and also give it to your parents for safekeeping.
- **LABEL everything.**
- **If your locker is far from your class** and hard to reach between classes, make sure to bring everything you need with you until you can return to your locker.
- **DON'T keep sweaty or smelly gym clothes in your locker.**

Maintain Your Neat Locker!

Throughout the school year, take time to maintain your locker's organization and neatness. Recycle papers, donate used books, clothing and supplies, and wipe all surfaces clean from any spilled items. Additionally, throw away trash and accumulated garbage.

Check School Rules!

Make sure to check school rules before you hang or attach anything to your locker.

My Brain, My Bible, My Academic Planner!

Being organized for class starts with an academic planner. Your academic planner is the bible for your school day. In it you should record homework assignments, test and quiz dates, extracurricular activity and anything related to your school life – both in and out of school.

Making Good Use of Your Planner

🖉 Write clearly.

🖉 Keep doodles to a minimum and certainly not in the space you need.

🖉 Enter assignments when announced on the correct date. Double check!

🖉 Record test and quiz dates.

🖉 Include sport/activity and all afterschool appointments.

🖉 Keep teachers'/friends' phone and email contact information if needed.

🖉 Check off assignments when complete.

🖉 Use a separate color ink to indicate homework, test/quiz dates and long term assignment due dates. Visual cues help the brain to process and categorize information quickly.

"I like to write and highlight the due date for long-tem assignments in my planner - not only do I know when something is assigned; I know when it is due too." —Megan S.

Keeping My Notes And Related Class Work Organized – The Current Stuff.

Keeping your class notes and related handouts, assignments, tests and quizzes organized can be done by several different methods. What works best for you consistently will determine the method you choose. No matter which system you choose, the goal is to keep work organized long term. Try to pick one system for organization and use it for all classes. Here are a few methods to choose from:

Using A 3-Ring Binder As Your Master Organizer

A three ring binder is the perfect system for at-school organization. It provides one central place for notes, handouts, assignments, and returned tests and quizzes. Additionally, it is a flexible system: you can customize the number of sections and tabs, adding additional paper as needed.

There are some key items it should contain:

1. Academic Planner

2. Pen/Pencil Case

3. Class Syllabus

4. School/Teacher Contact Information

5. Class Notes (you may further choose to divide this section by chapter or main topic)

6. Pocket Folders for:
   a. Notes/permission slips to go home/be handed in
   b. Homework to go home/handed in
   c. Current corrected homework, quizzes and tests that will be filed for studying later; eventually filed permanently or discarded

If you use a 3-ring binder as your master organizer, it should go to and from home and to every class each day so that you can record information and store/hand in items as necessary.

If you use this system, handouts can be 3-hole-punched and inserted directly into the note section they refer to. If not, all handouts can be stored in a tabbed section alone or in a pocket.

Separate Spiral Notebooks For Each Subject

Some kids prefer a single spiral notebook for each class. This is another way to neatly organize your school work. If this is your choice, make sure to use a spiral notebook that includes build-in pocket folders. If you buy a spiral notebook without pocket folders, make sure to purchase a separate pocket folder to coordinate with each notebook. Keep current information in the pocket dividers contained in the notebook and use extra pocket dividers for additional storage. The downside to using a spiral notebook is that you are unable to add pages unless you staple or tape the information to the preceding or following page. The bonus to using spiral notebooks is that they are smaller and easier to handle.

Using Plastic Or Accordion Folders For Storage

Plastic folders are popular in the lower elementary grades because there is little information, books, or notebooks needed yet. A single plastic folder allows for all of the child's school day information to be placed in one location for going to and from school. The teacher is able to collect homework and notes in one plastic folder per student and then place the next set of homework and notes in the same folder to send home. In essence, it is a two-way conduit between parent and teacher. For older students, the plastic folder can be used for subjects that produce a few loose papers, but not much more. The folder will keep papers well protected, but there is not a lot of storage room.

Accordion folders are another paper storage solution. They can be used in two ways: for multiple subjects or for a single subject. If you are using a single accordion folder for multiple subjects be mindful that it only expands a limited amount, so it is important that you maintain good secondary storage at home. You'll have to frequently move items that are not current. It is also important to note that the accordion folder will need to go with you from class to class along with your academic planner, books, and notebooks. If you are using a single accordion folder for each subject label the tabs.

Plastic folders and accordion folders, while an organizing option, are the most cumbersome.

Suggestions To Further Keep You Organized – Try it, You'll Like It!

- Date everything—homework, handouts, class notes, etc., it makes it easy to organize and keep track of items.

- Be creative: use color to identify subjects at a glance. Color code notebooks and related folders, and use a different color, when possible, to distinguish between assignment and activity type. (Example: Red = test/quiz, Blue = homework assignment, Green = paper or long term assignment and Black = non-academic activity.)

- Match your notebook colors to your home file storage system.

FROM BRAIN TO PAPER: LISTS

Why Make Lists?

Making lists can give you a sense of accomplishment. As you add items to your list, you can stop worrying about reminding yourself to do them. When you cross items off your list, you are getting things done, and the list becomes smaller. Look what you've accomplished! You are becoming more productive and feel a sense of satisfaction with yourself.

Seeing What You Need To Do:

Making lists also allows you to visualize what that needs to get done. It's always important to prioritize tasks logically and efficiently. Writing it all down and numbering the order of importance will reduce or eliminate wasted time.

Lists To Start:

✔ **A "Now" or "To Do" list:** Use this list for items that need to be done NOW, today. For example: list phone calls that need to be made, emails that need to be sent, homework errands that need to be completed, doctors appointments that are scheduled, after school classes and sports, and of course "homework"—not each individual assignment as this will be in your planner, but just a time slot for homework itself.

✔ **A "Soon" list:** This list is for items that do not need to get done today, but soon. For example, you need to go to the soccer store to buy new cleats before the soccer season begins, or you have to go to the library to check out a list of summer reading books.

✔ **A "Someday" list** (Goals): Use this list for long-term goals and rainy day activities. For example sorting camp or school pictures or researching summer teen travel programs. This list is for all the not "right now" or pressing items.

✔ **A "Fix-It" list:** Use this list for items that require fixing. For example, your iPod is not working and you need to take it to the Apple Store. While it is important to get this done, it is not something you need to do today, nor is it something for soon or someday. The "fix-it" association helps you remember that it needs to be taken care of.

✔ **A School Planner**, aka Academic Planner: Use your Academic Planner to account for all homework assignments, test and quiz dates, and project/writing assignment dates. Your planner is not a list in the traditional sense, but rather more like a calendar with notes. It should go with you to all classes and come home with you each night. It is your guide to getting that evening's homework done, planning for upcoming test/quiz study time, managing tasks to be completed for project and writing assignments, and as a guide to preparing for the next school day.

Prioritizing your lists is the key to working efficiently and getting the most accomplished in the least amount of time.

MY SPACE, MY ORGANIZED SPACE...

A Neat, Organized Space Of Your Own

The secret to being organized is giving everything a designated place—from sports equipment, backpacks, clothing, cell phones, and keys. All of these should be grouped together with like items. If everything is put where it should be, it's simple to find! Getting out of the house each morning is a piece of cake if you spend little time spent looking around for the, "Oops," where is my...

Your room, closet and desk are your responsibility. The better they are organized; the better will be the use of your time. Given the hectic schedule of most children, any time lost attempting to find items is lost and irretrievable. Ergo, keep your personal spaces organized!

Your Room

Room size varies, so it's great to make the most of the space you have. Try to understand what functions your space needs to accommodate, for example, sleeping, homework, music, art, or exercise—and at the same time, consider what can be accommodated elsewhere. Make an honest evaluation and then you can weed out functions/activities you don't need in your room. If you share a room, this is a great way to work together with a sibling.

It's always important to arrange furniture and items in your room so that related items are together. If for example, you play guitar; then your instrument, music stand, music books and amplifier should occupy the same space.

Your Closet

In your closet, group similar items together.

Stuff You Can Fold:

Jeans, shorts, tank tops, long sleeve shirts and short sleeve shirts should each have their own pile or shelf if you have a lot of these items and you have enough closet space. They can also be placed in a dresser drawer if your closet is too small. Similarly, underwear and socks should have separate spaces. If you do not have drawer space for these items, use a labeled plastic storage bin and place on a shelf in the closet. To further organize your clothes, you can arrange similar items (shirts, slacks, jackets) by color.

Shoes:

Use shoe bins or hanging shoe bags as they provide greater storage in a smaller amount of space. Try not to pile shoes on the floor.

Stuff That Hangs:

Use hooks on the back of the closet door for belts and scarves or other small hanging items. Similarly you can add a few wall hooks for bags, purses, baseball caps or other hats. Use a tie rack or fold ties nicely and place in a drawer or in a plastic bin on a shelf. If you hang ties on a hook, it can leave crease marks.

Seasonal Items:

To store seasonal items, such as winter gloves, bathing suits, or camp clothing, use labeled plastic storage containers and place them on the top shelves of your closet. You can also get a set of plastic drawers (normally on wheels) that can be placed in the closet for additional storage. Switch out these items as the seasons change. And for fun, take a snapshot of a clothing item and tape it to the front of the storage container so you know what is contained within.

AMY'S ROOM AND CLOSET TIPS:

- Items used daily should be easy to reach; grab and go!

- Place seasonal items in labeled plastic storage bins on top closet shelf or under bed. Bed risers can be purchased to raise the level of the bed making more storage space beneath.

- Keep similar items grouped together.

- Small plastic bins, colorful photo storage boxes, and colorful stacking cubes are great organizers for smaller items.

- Strategically hang hooks in the closet for extra hanging storage.

Your Desk

Refer back to Homework Space – Declutter My Desk for tips on keeping your desk space organized and homework ready.

Student Notes:

APPENDIX 1:

EXTRA! EXTRA! – BACK TO SCHOOL SHOPPING

Plan Ahead!

Take an inventory of what you child currently has including school supplies and clothing that fits. Put aside the non-fitting clothes for donation, or hand them down to a sibling or friend. If your child goes to a "uniform" school, you may want to see if they have a used clothing program. When you receive the list of required supply items, compare it to your inventory of what items you already have on hand. Chances are you may have leftover pens and pencils from the prior year. The same for scissors, rulers and calculators. These items seldom go out of style – however, depending on the math course being taken, a different model calculator may be required.

By taking inventory, by default, you are able to create a list of what is needed.

Time To Shop!

Many stores offer coupons or have sales during back to school time. Check flyers for bargains and keep coupons and clipped advertisements in an envelope in your purse so when you are headed to the store, you are armed to get the best deal.

Make the most of your shopping day. Plan your store stops so that you are working efficiently. Make a list of the shops you need to visit and then number them according to your driving route that allows you to avoid back-tracking to the extent possible.

Keeping all back to school shopping receipts in one place makes for easy returns or exchanges. I use a simple white envelope and label it "back to school" to store all the receipts. When making purchases be mindful of return policies, not all stores are the same.

Keep in mind, for young children, it can be easier to purchase and bring home clothing to check for fit, or to use as a guide for catalog or on-line shopping, but as noted, be especially mindful of return policies. If you are taking the little ones for a full day of shopping, make sure to plan lunch or snacks into your day. The down time and replenishment will help to keep them, and you, going.

Cross items off the list as you go and add items you may have forgotten as well. I typically make my list in one color ink and scratch off/add in another. When I come home, I rewrite my list for the next outing and organize again by driving route and store.

It is not necessary to wait for all supplies and clothing to be purchased to start organizing. Pick a spot in the home - we like to use the dining room table - to lay out school supplies and start labeling and sorting for each child/class. Clothing should be tried on as soon as possible and the items that need to be returned or exchanged placed near the door so that they are easily visible and ready to go. All clothing that is to be kept should be washed and put away in closets and drawers without delay. Place clothing items that are used most where they are easily accessible. For example; if the school has a dress code, these clothing items should be placed where they are reachable, while weekend attire and fancy dress items should be placed more remotely.

Note
• Dress your child in layers as the temperature throughout the day may change.

APPENDIX 2:

EXTRA! EXTRA! – BACK TO "NEW" SCHOOL AT ANY AGE

The first day of school can be stressful for students, especially if they are attending a new school. Here are a few tips to help you and your student start off with a smooth transition.

Before the first day, contact the school to schedule a tour of the school building and facilities to familiarize your child with the layout. Locate classrooms, bathrooms, school office(s), gymnasiums, the lunchroom and the infirmary. Even if you've had a tour of the school at the time you were looking (if you are relocating to a new area), it's always a good idea to do it again just before the school year starts up. Knowing the locations of these rooms and areas will make your child more comfortable in their new surroundings.

If possible, set up an appointment with your child's homeroom teacher or student advisor (if they do not have a homeroom teacher). If this is not possible, arrange to have a telephone conversation before the first day of school. Use this time to discuss your child's personality, his or her ability to make new friends, and any fears your child may have coming into the school as a new student, or anything else you deem important.

Try to arrange a get together with one of the children in your child's class in the week or two prior to the start of school. This child may or may not end up being your child's closest friend, however having a familiar face to say "hi" and make small talk will do wonders to calm first day jitters.

Make sure all summer assignments are complete and organized in your child's backpack. A week prior to the start of school confirm that all assignments are complete. Should there be more to get done, your child has ample, non-rushed, time to complete the work.

At home, the night before the big day, pack back packs and additional school supplies. Decide on first day outfits and lay clothing out. Place backpack near the door so that the morning is quick, easy and stress free. Get your child to bed early so that he or she can get a good night's rest and plan to awaken a few minutes early in the morning. This will allow for extra time, if needed, to get ready and out the door.

Most important, make sure that your child eats a healthy breakfast and reinforce to them that it will be a great day. Head for the bus or car pool with a big smile, assuring your child that there will be new friends and an exciting fun-filled day ahead.

10235022R0

Made in the USA
Lexington, KY
08 July 2011